Y0-BZV-305

Genre **Expository Text**

Essential Question
What contributions were made by early civilizations?

Lost in Time

by Howard Raymond

Introduction 2

Chapter 1
Indus, Lost and Found 4

Chapter 2
People of the Rivers 7

Chapter 3
City Life 10

Chapter 4
Art and Culture 13

Conclusion 16

Respond to Reading 18

PAIRED READ Words from the Past 19

Glossary 22

Index 23

Focus on Social Studies 24

Introduction

Imagine holding in your hand a tiny clay statue that no one has touched for more than 4,000 years. Or imagine exploring a dark and mysterious ancient fort. An experience like this might cause you to ask questions about the lives of the people who created such things. What was the purpose of the clay statue? Why did the people build that fort?

It's the job of **archaeologists** to ask such questions and to study artifacts and historical sites to try to determine the answers. Often they will make discoveries about ancient cultures that relate to objects or technology we use today.

One civilization that archaeologists have been studying for more than a century is the Indus civilization, named after the main river in the area. Thousands of years ago, the Indus civilization stretched over most of modern-day Pakistan, as well as parts of Afghanistan and northern India.

Then this mighty civilization died out and disappeared. In fact, it lay forgotten for more than three millennia, or 3,000 years.

Archaeological **excavations** provide yearly yields of new information that often confirms previously held theories. However, archaeologists still have numerous questions about the Indus civilization.

Different styles of small clay carts, some even including drivers, have been found in excavations in the Indus region. Archaeologists think these artifacts were probably toys.

How is it possible that a civilization that covered such an extensive area could be lost for so long? Unlike more famous civilizations, such as those of Mesopotamia and ancient Egypt, the Indus civilization didn't feature large buildings or monuments. Over time, its ruins were almost completely buried and lay undisturbed and undiscovered.

There are numerous theories about what caused the decline of the Indus civilization. One hypothesis is that it was caused by repeated flooding and other changes in the weather.

One established fact concerns how this lost civilization came to be rediscovered. The answer, as often happens with such breakthroughs, is that it was found accidentally.

The Indus Civilization

Oxcarts have been used for centuries and are still commonly used for transportation in the Indus region.

Although archaeologists have been working on excavations at Indus Valley sites for nearly 100 years, much remains to unearth. However, it wasn't archaeologists who made the original discovery of the lost Indus civilization.

The unlikely discoverer of Harappa (huh-RA-puh), the first great Indus city to be found, was a British army deserter, James Lewis, in 1826. Calling himself Charles Masson and posing as an engineer, he came across the ruins of a **citadel**, a large walled area, in what is now Pakistan. Although people still lived in a nearby village, neither Masson nor the villagers realized what an astounding archaeological site lay beneath them.

In the 1870s, another Englishman, archaeologist Alexander Cunningham, discovered an exquisitely carved small stone at the same site. Cunningham studied the stone and described it in his writings, but he didn't know what it was used for or what the mysterious inscription meant.

This cylinder seal from Harappa may have been used to create an impression on a two-dimensional surface, such as wet clay or wax.

From about the 1850s until 1947 the British ruled what is now India and Pakistan. The British established and extended transportation, including a railway network. In 1856, engineers laying the tracks came across the ruins at Harappa, which contained uniformly sized bricks. The railroad workers utilized these bricks in constructing the bed for the rails. Brick robbers also used the bricks for house building. By 1872, the upper layer of bricks at the site had been destroyed.

Nowadays removing artifacts from sites without permission is prohibited by international law. This is because we now recognize how much we can learn from even the smallest discoveries.

While many explorers in the past were hunting for treasures, such as gold and jewelry from ancient tombs, modern archaeologists are more interested in learning about how people lived. Therefore, a chipped cooking pot could yield as much information as an item of greater material value.

Excavation can be very slow, hot, and tedious work. An archaeological site may have numerous layers, showing changes over time in an area.

By the 1860s, the British rulers had come to appreciate the importance of ancient sites, and they established the Archaeological Survey of India to help protect unique cultural monuments. Today's archaeologists often work on modern construction sites to ensure that irreparable damage isn't caused.

The ruins at the Indus site were extensive, and in 1920, the proper excavation of Harappa began. Indian Daya Ram Sahni and Englishman John Marshall supervised the excavations at Harappa. Marshall believed that the Indus civilization was older than any others previously known. In 1922, another archaeologist, R. D. Banerji, made a further exciting discovery. He found evidence of an even bigger city in the Indus Valley, called Mohenjo-Daro *(moh-HEN-joh DAHR-oh)*. With two large cities to study, archaeologists were able to start piecing together facts about life in this fascinating ancient civilization.

The citadel was an important gathering place as well as a shelter in times of danger. It was once thought that the city's end was due to an invasion, but this theory is debated.

CHAPTER 2

People of the Rivers

Archaeologists found evidence that people grew crops and herded cattle, sheep, and goats at a site called Mehrgarh *(MEER-gah)*, located in the Indus Valley region. Archaeologists believe that this site existed before the Indus civilization. Because of this, they think that the Indus people were farmers as far back as 6000 or 7000 B.C.E.

Over several millennia, these people gradually changed from being farmers and herders to being city dwellers. Evidence suggests that the Indus civilization was at its peak from about 2500 B.C.E. to about 1700 B.C.E.

Archaeologists have asked, what made this giant transformation possible? The answer is surprisingly simple. When the Indus people are compared with two more famous civilizations that existed at the same time, those of Egypt and Mesopotamia, a common link is found. These civilizations flourished in part because of their close proximity to rivers. Water is the lifeblood of civilization.

Calculating Time

Time in the Western world is commonly centered on year 1. The time before that date is called B.C.E., which stands for Before the Common Era. The time after this date is called C.E., meaning in the Common Era.

In calculating ancient time before year 1, it's necessary to think backward. The larger the number, the older the time period.

The Indus cities developed on the floodplains of the Indus River and another great river that has dried up, the Hakra *(HAK-rah)*, also known as the Sarasvati *(SAR-uhs-vuh-tee)*.

Over the centuries, floods along these two rivers transported layers of rich, gritty soil, called silt, down from the hills to the plains. The silt remained when the floodwaters receded, and it made the land of the plains very fertile.

However, these rivers flooded regularly and could cause great devastation. Crops could be depleted or destroyed, buildings and equipment carried away, and people and animals drowned.

The Indus people learned to recognize when flooding was likely to occur. They prepared themselves by moving to higher ground and constructing the walls of their citadels to direct floodwaters away from their cities.

The crops that Indus farmers cultivated suggest that the Indus people ate a healthful diet that included wheat, barley, fruit, and legumes, foods still eaten in modern times.

Along with growing crops, the Indus people were able to **domesticate** dogs, cats, cattle, sheep, goats, and chickens. They even domesticated the elephant!

Because floods were regular and predictable, people planned for them by building on raised platforms.

If food is plentiful, people can settle down in one place instead of needing to move around to find pasture for their flocks and fertile land to grow crops. With repeated good harvests, settlements get bigger. More importantly, not everyone has to work in the fields or herd animals.

The successes of farmers allow others in the community to share the food that is produced. Specialization develops from a variety of different skills, such as toolmaking or weaving, and an income can be derived. Communal life in towns and villages becomes stronger and more varied. Finally the stage is set for a key transformation: towns turn into cities!

Traditional methods of irrigation utilizing canals are still practiced in rural India and Pakistan.

Ancient Cotton

Archaeologists believe that the Indus people were among the first to grow cotton and transform it into cloth. Once cotton was picked from the field, all the seeds, hulls, and debris had to be separated from the white, fluffy part of the plant. Then the cotton had to be spun into thread. The thread was then woven into cloth, and the cloth was dyed. Thousands of years later, cotton is still important to the economies of India and Pakistan.

Major Cities

Two of the most populated cities that developed in the Indus civilization were Harappa and Mohenjo-Daro. Each city covered an area of about one square mile and had a population of as many as 50,000 people.

Despite being about 400 miles (644 kilometers) apart, the two cities were of a similar design and were both built from brick. The design would have helped the cities deal with the pressures of an increasingly large number of people.

Both cities were divided into a lower part, where most people lived, and a citadel on higher ground. Although called citadels, these weren't forts in the traditional sense. They included a range of different spaces. Each citadel contained spaces that could have been a great hall and either a **granary**, an administrative center, or possibly a temple.

The lower housing areas of the cities were impressive for their straight, wide streets and orderly grid design. That type of neat, logical layout is common in modern cities, but is uncommon in ancient ones.

Layout of the Mohenjo-Daro Citadel

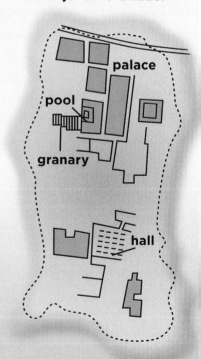

10

The sophisticated **sanitation** system was another amazingly advanced feature. Most houses had brick-floored bathrooms with drainage pipes. Some bathrooms had running water. Even today, there are many areas around the world that don't have such a luxury.

Government and Society

Little is known about the Indus rulers. It is not known whether the Indus people were ruled by governors, rich merchants, or religious leaders. It is possible that the leaders held all three roles.

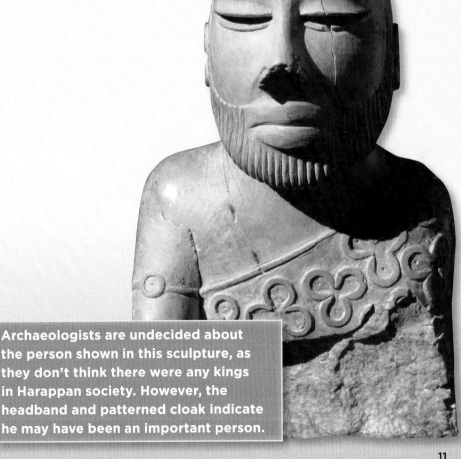

Archaeologists are undecided about the person shown in this sculpture, as they don't think there were any kings in Harappan society. However, the headband and patterned cloak indicate he may have been an important person.

There are no large burial sites full of treasures like the sites that were constructed for pharaohs in Egypt. Such tombs can indicate the status of the person buried there. The absence of grand burial sites makes some archaeologists think that Indus society could have been more **egalitarian** than other ancient civilizations. However, the Indus civilization still included divisions of society: a ruling class, tradespeople and **artisans**, and laborers.

Another remarkable aspect of the Indus civilization is that there is little to suggest there was any violence or military organization. Though battles and armies played a major role in other ancient civilizations, it seems that life for Indus people was mostly peaceful. They appear to have lived in a harmonious, communal fashion.

Because the cities and towns in the Indus region are generally very similar in appearance, it suggests that there was an effective communication network across the region. The town planners and engineers would have had the ability to spread the word about their impressive advances, such as their system of weights and measures. This is a way of measuring things using standard units, like an inch or a pound in the United States. A good standard measurement system was important for trade. Archaeologists believe it could even have been used in collecting taxes. It is an important development that is still used by societies today.

Unlike other ancient civilizations, the Indus civilization had no grand palaces, temples, pyramids, statues, or trappings of wealth. The cities were large and well laid out, but deceptively plain and simple, with no elaborate architecture. Instead, it seems that Indus craftspeople poured their energy into making small, exquisite artworks.

Indus artifacts include a wide variety of toys and games, ornaments, figurines, and jewelry. The materials artisans used ranged from bone, shell, clay, and limestone to ivory, silver, and gold. In some cases, it is obvious how these artifacts would have been used. In other cases, it is puzzling, especially if the artifact portrays a person. Does it portray a real person? Did the person play a vital role in rituals or religious ceremonies? Or does the artifact represent a god or goddess?

Pottery is still a major art form in India. Indus pots date back as far as 5500 B.C.E. Some patterns used today still show the influence of Indus culture.

The Indus Seals

In the years after Alexander Cunningham found the little carved stone, many similar stones were found. These are called the Indus seals. Most of these seals show real or imaginary animals and include some form of writing. Archaeologists are frustrated by the shortness of the inscriptions on the 4,000 seals uncovered so far. Without finding longer texts, scientists won't be able to decode the writing.

The mythical unicorn is the animal most commonly depicted on the Indus seals. Real animals depicted include elephants, tigers, antelopes, and rhinoceroses.

The seals could have been pressed in wax or wet clay, which after drying could have been attached to bundles of **merchandise**.

There is still disagreement about the main purpose of the seals. One possibility is that they were used in business and trade as a kind of stationery, perhaps to mark ownership of goods or to indicate who produced them. Or perhaps they served another purpose—maybe as symbols for different clans in Indus society. No one knows for sure.

DEA/G. NIMATALLAH/De Agostini/Getty Images

Trade

The Indus people were very successful traders. Their goods were transported as far as Mesopotamia, central Asia, and along the Persian Gulf. The evidence for this is that Indus seals have been found in these places. Indus people also imported copper, gold, silver, and precious gems from other regions.

In the Indus culture, jewelry was popular with both men and women.

Using oxcarts or pack animals to transport goods over land would have been very slow and time consuming. However, the rivers acted like highways from the mountains to the ocean. They helped Indus traders spread their goods and commodities throughout the region and further afield.

Development of Indus Civilization

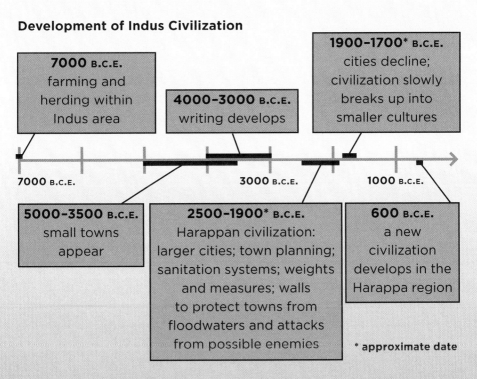

7000 B.C.E.
farming and herding within Indus area

4000–3000 B.C.E.
writing develops

1900–1700* B.C.E.
cities decline; civilization slowly breaks up into smaller cultures

7000 B.C.E.   3000 B.C.E.   1000 B.C.E.

5000–3500 B.C.E.
small towns appear

2500–1900* B.C.E.
Harappan civilization: larger cities; town planning; sanitation systems; weights and measures; walls to protect towns from floodwaters and attacks from possible enemies

600 B.C.E.
a new civilization develops in the Harappa region

* approximate date

Conclusion

From farming to city life, from business to art, the Indus civilization contributed a number of advances that are part of modern daily life. Some remain relatively unchanged, while others have been expanded or adapted.

Theories about what happened to the Indus change over time as new evidence appears. Archaeologists think the reason for their decline might be the same factor that caused them to flourish—the power of rivers. There may have been a big flood, or the opposite may be true: the rivers may have dried up or changed course.

Although the cities died away and eventually disappeared, people continued to live in towns and villages in the area. This meant a huge shift in their lifestyle, but the Indus didn't forget their culture. Some archaeologists argue that the achievements of later Indian civilizations were made possible by the Indus. At the very least, Indus ideas and innovations influenced the new peoples who colonized the region.

The citadel at Mohenjo-Daro is not a simple fort, but a raised mound at the eastern side of the city containing different buildings. The mound gave protection against flooding, although water damage is still an issue at the site today.

The city of Mohenjo-Daro covers a large area, and much of it is yet to be excavated.

Despite all the uncertainties, people today are very aware of the significance of the Indus civilization. In 1980, Mohenjo-Daro was added to the list of UNESCO (United Nations Educational, Scientific, and Cultural Organization) World Heritage sites. This organization protects places that have "outstanding universal value." With the support of governments around the world, it works to protect such sites so archaeologists can continue attempting to solve its many mysteries.

Summarize

Use important details from *Lost in Time* to summarize what you have learned about the Indus and their contributions to civilization. Your graphic organizer might help you.

Problem	Solution

Text Evidence

1. How do you know that *Lost in Time* is an expository text? Identify the text features. GENRE

2. What problems do archaeologists face in trying to understand how ancient societies lived? PROBLEM AND SOLUTION

3. Look at page 4. The word *discovered* comes from the Latin roots *dis*, meaning "opposite," and *cooperire*, meaning "to cover." How does this help you understand the meaning of *discovered*? LATIN ROOTS

4. Identify a problem that people living on floodplains in ancient times had to face. Write about the problem and how it was solved. WRITE ABOUT READING

Compare Texts

Read about how an ancient civilization has contributed to literature.

Words from the Past

Civilizations have risen and fallen over the millennia, but much of their art still exists. An important piece of ancient writing from India has survived. It is called *The Mahabharata* and was written over hundreds of years, starting about 1,500 years after the decline of the Indus civilization. It is one of the longest poems in the world, with almost 100,000 verses spread over 18 books. It has been passed down over the ages and translated into different languages. It has also been adapted into other forms, such as theater, dance, and music. An Indian television series based on the epic poem lasted 94 episodes and had an enormous audience.

The versions of selected verses from *The Mahabharata* on the following pages are based on a late-nineteenth-century English translation of the original Sanskrit text.

Where is time
> when the grass is new?
> or the snow is deep?

Where is time
> when we're asleep?

Is time really something we can keep?

Time marches on
and is not held back
past present future
right on track

But the gift of time
—and here's the thrill—
you make of each moment
what you will

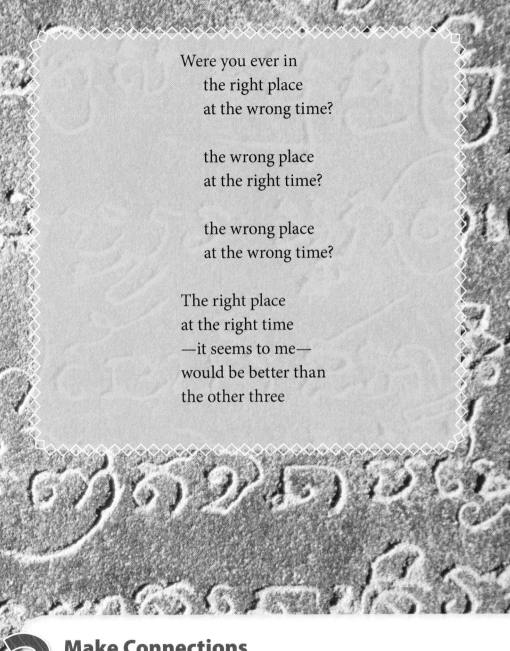

Were you ever in
   the right place
   at the wrong time?

   the wrong place
   at the right time?

   the wrong place
   at the wrong time?

The right place
at the right time
—it seems to me—
would be better than
the other three

Make Connections

How has *The Mahabharata* contributed to later
works of art? ESSENTIAL QUESTION

What have archaeologists found out about the lives
of ancient people by studying the Indus civilization
and *The Mahabharata*? TEXT TO TEXT

Glossary

archaeologists *(ahr-kee-AHL-uh-jists)* scientists who study people of the past by examining sites and artifacts *(page 2)*

artisans *(AHR-tuh-zuhns)* skilled craftspeople who make ornaments and/or utensils by hand *(page 12)*

citadel *(SIT-uh-del)* enclosed, walled area or fort, usually on higher ground overlooking a town or city *(page 4)*

domesticate *(duh-MES-ti-kayt)* to tame a species of wild animal so it can be used for meat, milk, wool, or other products *(page 8)*

egalitarian *(ee-gal-uh-TER-ee-uhn)* no class of people are considered to be better than any other *(page 12)*

excavations *(eks-kuh-VAY-shuhns)* the process of mapping out and digging at archaeological sites *(page 2)*

granary *(GRAH-nuh-ree)* a building for storing grain *(page 10)*

merchandise *(MURH-chuhn-dighs)* goods for sale or trade *(page 14)*

sanitation *(sa-nuh-TAY-shuhn)* the process of making things sanitary; for example, removal of sewage and trash *(page 11)*

Index

art and culture, *13–16, 19*

city planning, *10–13*

cotton, *9*

Cunningham, Alexander, *4, 14*

Egypt, *3, 7, 12*

flooding, *8, 15, 16*

government and society, *11, 12*

Hakra or Sarasvati River, *3, 8*

Harappa, *3–6, 15*

India, *2, 3, 5, 9, 13, 16, 19*

Indus River, *2, 3, 8*

jewelry, *13, 15*

Mahabharata, The, 19–21

Masson, Charles, *4*

Mehrgarh, *3, 7*

Mesopotamia, *3, 7, 15*

Mohenjo-Daro, *3, 6, 10, 16, 17*

Pakistan, *2–5, 9*

seals, *4, 14, 15*

Focus on Social Studies

Purpose To compare the Indus with other cultures and understand how being close to a large river had benefits for each

What to Do

Many ancient cultures have grown up around rivers. Having water nearby had many benefits.

Step 1 Work with a partner or in a group. Reread the sections of *Lost in Time* that discuss the Indus and Hakra rivers. Make notes on the benefits and the problems that resulted from having these rivers close by.

Step 2 Now research other ancient civilizations that developed near large rivers—ancient Egypt by the Nile river, and Mesopotamia between the Tigris and Euphrates rivers. Research how and why ancient communities developed along these rivers. What were the benefits? What were the problems and how did the societies living there solve them?

Step 3 Make a chart with the headings "Benefits" and "Problems". List your information under these headings.

Step 4 Present your chart to the class. Describe how the benefits of living by a river were enjoyed by the people of the civilizations you researched and how the problems were solved.